Alphalexia

poems by

Barbra Nightingale

Finishing Line Press
Georgetown, Kentucky

Alphalexia

Copyright © 2017 by Barbra Nightingale
ISBN 978-1-63534-138-6 First Edition
All rights reserved under International and Pan-American Copyright Conventions. No part of this book may be reproduced in any manner whatsoever without written permission from the publisher, except in the case of brief quotations embodied in critical articles and reviews.

ACKNOWLEDGMENTS

Grateful thanks go out to the following for first publication:
Sliver of Stone   "A", "B," "C," "D," and "E"
Red Booth Review   "G," "H," "I," "J" and "K"
Heart Mind Zone "T"
Many thanks also go to my personal poetry gurus: Denise Duhamel, Gary Kay, and Paul Saluk.

Publisher: Leah Maines

Editor: Christen Kincaid

Cover Art: Debbie Neale—www.clickncolour.com

Author Photo: DOWNTOWN PHOTO

Cover Design: Elizabeth Maines

Printed in the USA on acid-free paper.
Order online: www.finishinglinepress.com
         also available on amazon.com

Author inquiries and mail orders:
Finishing Line Press
P. O. Box 1626
Georgetown, Kentucky 40324
U. S. A.

Table of Contents

A 1
B 2
C 3
D 4
E 5
F 6
G 7
H 8
I 9
J 10
K 11
L 12
M 13
N 14
O 15
P 16
Q 17
R 18
S 19
T 20
U 21
V 22
W 23
X 24
Y 25
Z 26

This book is dedicated to my personal poetry gurus and to all my friends and family who have given me much strength and encouragement.

A

This is where it begins. First
and foremost: singular, anonymous,
first in everything but tone,
where it is sixth, depending
on the scale. Everything depends
on scale. Life hanging
       in the balance,
a finite number or amount
such as a day, a month, a year.
Yes, even a lifetime. How much
is that? An actuary could tell you,
down to the tenth, but still it wouldn't
describe all the breaths
it took to get there, balanced
on the precipice, the tip
of those scales.

B

How round, how buxom!
No wonder bosom begins with B.
Say it aloud, it's a noun, a verb,
a grade less than perfect.
Observe its curves!
How could it ever be second rate?
Slip your lips around its minions
(Babel, babble, bacchanal)
such a gathering of hosts!
All up to their ears in backwash,
bogarting the bottle as if they owned
the world, from Baker Street to Bali—
not one baboon in sight.

C

Remember Crispin sailing on an open C?
It is only now, I realize how similar C is to sea,
and that I do not suffer from cacography
except in sleight of hand.
The roll and pitch of that arc
a sideways wave hello or goodbye.
Who is to say? When the nights are clear
no clouds hang low, and stars console the moon.
Who waits in chastened corners of darkness?
Who is it out there, alone, baying to the sky?
Who could tell a chord from a choral,
a church from a church key?

D

Dance! Death says, *Dance!*
and dance we do—
up, down, around, around.
Desperate steps to ward it off,
hands raised, fingers crossed.
But Death is always lurking.
Hear it rumble: a deep bassoon
from under the diaphragm.
Capital, it looks pregnant,
lowercase—backward, dark, full
of portent, looming endings—
all the words for dead.
Sooner than we think.

E

Like someone caught a mouse
or swallowed something bitter.
A sound you never forget: elemental.
Think about life as an electron
always following on the fringe,
attracting opposites, repelling
sameness, commonalities,
evidence of evisceration.
Eternally condemned like a bad memory
or a taste you can't spit out.

F

Failure. Fornication. Faith.
There's a threesome! Effing
mouthful of euphemisms.
Mirror, mirror on the wall,
Who's the fairest of them all?
Effing bloody right, you are.
A fairy tale complete
with fanfare and farce,
drama and flourish, as if the fairies
gathered to dance in the dust—
a fictitious five-alarm fire
kicked up by their sparks.
Incandescent, fibrilant.
Fundamental as fractured rain.

G

Genetically speaking, we're all over the map,
moving up or down, notch by notch,
one gene at a time, generating myriad codes
from a pool as generative as tadpoles.
We morph from gamete to General,
genus to genius, gullible to galled.
Look at it: complexly figured, all curves and angles.
A geometric anomaly.
Is a glow-worm so different from a grub?
A Guava from a gourd?
Do grudges mutate generationally
(like the Hatfields and McCoys)?
Or do they only gyrate wedges between us?
In the general sense of the world,
our gilded grievances aren't worth a gigabyte of time.
Time to trade up.

H

Holy hell, he hiccoughed, how hateful
hypocrites can be, how hermetic
in nature, how homogenously hindsightful.
Take all those beefy rhetoricians, choosing
and changing sides.
Give me a hypothesis, hypothetical
or not, hysterics will be spinning
on saucers in hypnotic trances.
But what the heck.
It's only politics, you say?

I

Imagined:
Idealist
Ideologue
Idiot
Ingenious
Ignorant
Ill-tempered
Immune
Immodest
Implacable
Impulsive
Inarticulate
Independent
Innocent
Invisible
Aye, there's the rub!
If I am imagined,
What's there to see?

J

Jumping Jehosephats, Batman!
Just when I thought this would all be jabberwocky,
J sprang out like a jack-in-the-box unhinged,
grinning like a jack-o-lantern, the Joker
all green and jacked up on some kind of juice.
I'm no Jungian judge of character,
but that jitterbug has one helluva junked out mind.
No telling what turns a Judah jubilant or a Joseph jocular.
Harder to imagine Batman himself
having a jolly old time, dour as he is from hanging
upside down most of his life.
Even our heroes have some sort of jitters.
Watch out for jokes and falling rocks.
Let's get the jetsam outta here!

K

K for potassium, my best friend's name,
for karat, a thousand, ka-ching!
Such a harsh sound in the value of things.
K is iconic: Kindle and killer bees,
Krypton, Kleenex, Captain Kidd.
Did you know there are dozens
of variant spellings for Kaballah?
If you can't spell it, it has no name,
known only by rumor and mystics
who can conjure empty space,
exotic place names for where
we've never been: Klondike, Kyoto, Katmandu.
What is knowledge but the absence of innocence?
The filling of a brain with facts.
Did you know Katzenjammer means hangover
and a kittiwake is a gull, hiding in the cliffs
up north, feeding on a cold, grey sea?
From kitsch to kazoo, our karma is calling.

L

A lamellicorn is a scarab
and a lamellibranch is a mollusk.
Now what do beetles and mussels
have in common besides their skin?
Perhaps we should start calling people
lamellicorns instead of overly sensitive.
In fact, we should launch a movement,
lament the loss of all the words
we never knew, never exchanged
over a lemonade or a latte last night.
The truth is, literally that out of tens of thousands
of words, less than a third are commonly used.
The rest lie moldering in textbooks, dictionaries,
technical manuals or botanists' guides, barely
crossing anyone's literal lips since first
they were uttered. Oh, for the lasciviousness
of wanton words! Let's hear them bantered about
like badminton birdies just for the pleasure,
the joy of the thwack!

M

Mothers, mothering, motherly, something
failed not once but twice over two generations.
Must be missing the maternal mitochondrial link.
I'm not alone: millions of mothers
should not have been: multicultural, multifaceted,
multifarious multitudes besieged by misogynists
and feminists alike. All boys should memorize:
> My mother is a woman.
> My mother is my friend.
> Women are my friends.

Maybe then the mayhem would cease.
Mix and mingle! Modify your life!
If you're going to make movies,
make them melodious. Make them with meaning.

N

Nothing beats n—the printer's dash,
the one that joins not separates, a hyphen
nascent and nappy, niggling neophytes
to newborn writers unaware
of nuanced punctuation, the dark
and twisted sounds of consonants
impossibly pronounced: nahuatl
namaycush*, nainsook,** narwhal,
a mouthful of nonsense
we somehow understand: *no lo contender*
nole-me-tanger, persona non-grata.
N is for nonconformity at its best,
but there are those who would nip it
in the bud, nifty nomenclature
notwithstanding. No noodles, no nooky,
no nouveau cuisine, especially,
no nouveau riche. Ah, nihilism!

*namaycush=Lake trout
**nainsook=striped cotton

O

Oh. O. Ohhhhh.
Surprised, mournful, ominous.
Objective? No. Observant? Yes,
even oblique, but never obsequious,
no matter how it's spelled.
Think of the possibilities,
but don't obfuscate the issues.
The objective correlative is after all
merely effect, a solicitation
of emotion, open to suggestion,
interpretation, perhaps even
onomatopoeia, obscure unless
obsessed with sound, obdurate
in the belief that words do more
than signify: they *mean*.

P

Putanesca. I've always wanted
to say that word, roll it around,
taste it in my mouth, calorie free.
Ah, the olives, basil, rich cheese,
the peel of consonants a tart flavor
dripping from the tongue.
Ever notice how a Portobello
and penis are much the same shape?
The proclivity for phallic psychology
is prodigious. (Now there's a mouthful!
Pun intended.) But think!
Putting them all in the pan is pretty prophetic,
given the provocative nature of food.
However big the pot, the more precipitous
the balance. Beware over salting.
Pass the pepper, please.

Q

To arrive at Q
questioning, always questioning
the quest! One might say
I'm querulous, a queen-mother
impervious to query, but no,
I'm just another quirk, a tidbit
of humanity, a quarter note, quaking
in the book of life, queued
in line like everyone else.
Here, then, is the quotidian:
the quotient of two equals one.
How Quixotic!

R

R-E-S-P-E-C-T! Rah rah rah!
Rally on, you radiant regenerates.
I don't give a ratfish for rapport
with the enemy! Ah, but when reason
steps in, reality rattles its tail
like a rattlesnake ready to strike
and reassurance be damned,
we're fraternizing, like it or not.
Don't try to convince me
you're on the rebound, the rate
of recidivism is astonishing, given
our recombinant genetics,
our predilection for rectitude,
redemption, all that rational
jargon, rapid fired at the brain.
An attempt to reanimate our dead
cells, reconnoiter, regroup, reclaim.
It's redundancy, in the end,
that will do us in, redoubled effort
to a rhetoric of questionable result.
Does no one ever recite
Why? Why? Why?

S

I've always wanted to use "swizzle"
in a poem, with or without the stick.
I love the swish of the zz's, the tickle
on my tongue, the silly, salacious
sound, the silken way it slides
out of my mouth. It has
a certain swag, I suppose,
like using "stipple" instead of "speckle,"
or "swelter" instead of "sweat."
Ah, the joy of synonyms—
syntax heaven, the stuff
my dreams spin into life.

T

Tenacious T. Perfection, as in fits like a T.
Tuesday. Tablespoon. Teaspoon (oddly confusing).
Temperature, time, troy (as in weight)
ta for thanks, ta ta for goodbye.
What interesting geometry is T, all right angles
and imaginary triangles, extrapolated, bisected,
tacked to the wall. You don't need to be a tactician
to know its place (or yours) in this thrilling typography;
you don't need a tachymeter or a tachometer,
but you might need a tachyscope, because perception
as we know, depends upon
recognition, memory, a tactile sense of tension,
palpable as fruit, almost as intense as tantric sex
whose definition could not be found.
A non-existent taxonomy purported in the 60s
(or was it later?) to be the stairway to heaven,
but turned out to be just like the poem: tautological
for no reason other than it is. Though some might claim
tetrahydrocannabinol (certainly the longest word I know)
is a testimonial to this kind of thought, the truth is
thanotological thinking prompts me more to tomfoolery
than chemical or theoretical constructs, though I must admit
the temptation to torment often has tragic results.
Tripping through the Ts I came to trigeminal neuralgia,
(which is something I've actually had), right next to
trigonometry, which I've never gotten, but learned a
marvelous bit of trivia: triskaidekaphobia (the fear of 13),
now a close second for the longest word I know, which is
actually a lie, since antiestablishmentarianism is the longest
word I know. And that's the truth.

U

Ubiquitous u. Un- as in
undone, unpleasant,
undeserved, unfamiliar, a whole page
of un—negation extraordinaire,
except when it's unleashed,
uncaged, unbridled as in passion
or unerring judgment;
unconquered, which is the same
as triumphant with or without
ultimatums. One does not
need to be told for the umpteenth time
that urban sprawl is a blight
or the universe is expanding.
It must be time to hitch a ride
to Uranus or at least Uzbekistan
where one would hope the air
if not the brown water
won't set the uranium
counter to ticking like madness.
In that case, nothing to do
but throw back your head and howl,
your uvula undulating
all the way back to the good old U.S. of A.

V

Vagina. A concrete word if ever
I've seen one. Notice I didn't
vacillate and got it out of the way
right off the bat. I'll say it again:
Vagina, only because it's never
been a word I liked, actually,
rather awkward and harsh, but now
that I see it so prominent on the page,
it has a certain grace, a definite void
waiting to be filled, almost valiant
in its patience. But enough of virgins
vestal or not, verisimilitude aside,
look at the formation!
Take away the sex and it's all
sharp angles; suitable only
for planes and geese.

W

W is a workhorse. Just look at
those triple peaks, the valleys
waiting in the shadows
of the words: Who? What? Where?
and most of all, Why?
The whippoorwill's a plaintive bird,
its sound lonelier than sorrow.
This wacky world goes whizzing by
a whirling dervish in the dust
wailing like the wicked witch
melting in the water. Huzzah,
wassup? Come, all you witchy widows,
weave a basket of cares to wend
down the river, waste not the rain.
The whippoorwill's a plaintive bird,
its sound lonelier than sorrow.

X

X marks the spot,
designates a speaker,
a person, a rating,
a generation Xer,
an unknown quantity.
But such a paucity of words,
the last three letters, scarce
ten (x) pages among them.
And while I admit to xenophilia
(so many sounds delicious on the tongue),
I abhor xenophobia, welcoming
Xaviers and Xiaos to my table,
even X-men, should they drop in
to tap on the xylophone ever so lightly,
like an X-ray star in the irradiant night.

Y

There is no word for this curvy shape,
no geometry for y, barely a symbol.
Perhaps it's only a theory, a Y2K
invention, ephemera of modernity
meant to provoke us to yammer
Y? Y? Y? The question for
everything, the answer for nothing,
till we've had it up the yazoo.
Throw off the yoke and head
for the Wild Blue Yonder, the Yukon,
or at least Yosemite, with nothing
but a handful of yuan
and a song in our throats.
Yup. Yuk. Yeah!

Z

Zorro, right? That famous zig-
zag signature, fiery and swift
as Zeus who can transmogrify
into anything he chooses
in a zeptosecond, which is fitting
since anything with a prefix
starting with sex (as in sextillioneth)
would make the King happy,
eating grapes fed by hand.
But let's not get carried away
by the shine on his zoster—
he went from zealot to zombie
after that swan business, nothing
but a zonker in my book.
What he ought to have done
is find a garden, a zaftig plot of land
and practiced Zen.
A lot less grief (not to mention literature)
would have ensued,
and all the stories might have had
happier endings. Don't you agree?

Barbra Nightingale's poems have appeared in many journals and anthologies, such as *Rattle, Narrative Magazine* (Poem of the Week), *Gargoyle, Barrow Street, The Georgetown Review, CRIT Journal, The Apalachee Review, Calyx, Kalliope, Many Mountains Moving, Birmingham Review, Chatahoochee Review, The Comstock Review, Poetrybay.com, The Mississippi Review.com, The MacGuffin, Crosscurrents, The Kansas Quarterly, Cumberlands Poetry Journal, Passages North, The Florida Review, Coydog Review.* and several national anthologies including *City of Big Shoulders, The Liberal Media Made Me Do It, Florida in Poetry, Tigertail,* and *Glass Bottom Sky.*

Book Publications include:
- *Two Voices, One Past*, Yellow Jacket Press, 2010
- *Geometry of Dreams* (2009), Word Tech Editions, Ohio,
- *The Ex-Files* (2009) (online by Goss 183)
- *Greatest Hits* (June, 2000): chapbook, Pudding House Press
- *Singing in the Key of L* (June, 1999) won the 1999 Stevens Poetry Manuscript Award, NFSPS,Inc.
- *Lunar Equations* (1993), East Coast Editions, NY
- *Prelude to a Woman* (1986) Earthwise Publications, Miami
- *Lovers Never Die* (1981), Lieb/Schott Publications, IL

Barbra Nightingale is a professor emeritus from Broward College (Ft. Lauderdale), and Advisor Emeritus from Phi Theta Kappa. She lives, works, and plays in Hollywood, Florida, with her various two and four legged menagerie of family.

www.ingramcontent.com/pod-product-compliance
Lightning Source LLC
LaVergne TN
LVHW041515070426
835507LV00012B/1581